THOUGHTS ON U.S. FOREIGN POLICY TOWARD THE PEOPLE'S REPUBLIC OF CHINA

Ramon H. Myers

HOOVER INSTITUTION
on War, Revolution and Peace

Stanford University
1994

Essays in Public Policy No. 47

Copyright © 1994 by the Board of Trustees of the
    Leland Stanford Junior University

Material contained in this essay may be quoted with appropriate citation.

First printing, 1994

Manufactured in the United States of America

98 97 96 95 94   9 8 7 6 5 4 3 2 1

Library of Congress Cataloging-in-Publication Data

Myers, Ramon Hawley, 1929–
    Thoughts on U.S. foreign policy toward the People's Republic of China /
    Ramon H. Myers
        p. cm. — (Essays in public policy ; no. 47)
    Includes bibliographical references.
    ISBN 0-8179-5522-4
    1. United States—Foreign relations—China. 2. China—Foreign
    relations—United States. I. Title. II. Series.
JX1428.C6M94   1994   94–5583
327.73051—dc20   CIP

Executive Summary

For the past eight months the Clinton administration has been warning the leaders of the People's Republic of China (PRC) that unless demonstrable progress occurs in human rights, the U.S. government will have no choice but to deny the PRC most-favored nation status. This essay presents several arguments to refute this foreign policy stance.

First, the PRC is at a critical stage of economic reform, and trade expansion greatly helps these reforms as well as the U.S. economy; thus, linking trade policy to human rights is bad foreign policy. Second, three broad areas—economic relations, human rights, and weapons proliferation—are equally important for U.S.-PRC relations and deserve serious negotiations on an issue-by-issue basis, not through linkage. Finally, a nuanced foreign policy by the United States will give the PRC's leaders time and space to build a new economic and ideological marketplace that will facilitate East Asia's prosperity and stability. The PRC will then develop along the same trajectory as did its counterpart, the Republic of China on Taiwan, several decades ago.

THOUGHTS ON U.S. FOREIGN POLICY TOWARD THE PEOPLE'S REPUBLIC OF CHINA

Ever since the leaders of the People's Republic of China (PRC) violently suppressed the student-led political demonstrations on June 4, 1989, in Beijing, the United States has made the improvement of human rights in China a centerpiece, along with economic liberalization, of U.S. foreign policy toward the PRC.

For example, on May 28, 1993, President Clinton signed an executive order stating that the United States would extend the PRC's most-favored nation (MFN) status on the following conditions: the PRC must grant freedom of emigration to its people and comply with a 1992 bilateral agreement to end exports to the United States of products made with prison labor. The PRC must then demonstrate progress in five areas:[1]

- Adherence to the Universal Declaration of Human Rights
- Release of and accounting for political prisoners
- Humane treatment of prisoners
- Protection of Tibet's "distinctive religious and cultural heritage"
- Permitting international radio and television broadcasts into the PRC

On October 1, 1993, U.S. secretary of state Warren Christopher warned the foreign minister of the PRC that "his country risks losing favorable trade status with the United States if it does not make quick progress on human rights and arms issues."[2] Thus, within a span of four months, the U.S. government had twice threatened the PRC with foreign trade sanctions if its leadership did not change its policies and institutions. Although the U.S. government mentioned standards that the PRC government must comply with, neither the U.S. government nor human rights lobby groups have agreed on such standards.

At the November 19, 1993, meeting for Asian Pacific Economic Cooperation (APEC) in Seattle, Washington, President Clinton told the PRC's president, Jiang Zemin, that when the PRC and the United States "work together, we are a powerful force for security and economic progress" and that "abuses of civil liberties in China must not be ignored but must not be permitted to dominate the relationship." President Clinton concluded, however, that improvements in human rights were necessary for the continuation of the PRC's MFN status. President Jiang responded with a fifteen-minute monologue about the "importance of noninterference in the internal affairs of other states." The talks proved candid, but neither side made any concession.[3]

In January 1994 Jiang Zemin reportedly told former President George Bush, who was visiting Beijing, that "China was planning to take a number of unspecified steps to improve its human rights record in coming months."[4] Red Cross delegates visiting Beijing also reported that Chinese officials had indicated their intent "to open prisons and detention centers to Red Cross inspectors this year in what would be the first outside inspection in 45 years of Communist rule."[5] Even in the area of economic relations, China's finance minister informed U.S. Treasury secretary Lloyd Bentsen on his visit to Beijing that the PRC would allow some American and foreign banks to expand into some cities and accept deposits in Chinese currency.[6] The PRC leadership, then, appeared to be trying to break the impasse that seemed to form in November 1993 after the Clinton-Jiang meeting in Seattle.

But in early February the U.S. State Department issued its annual report on human rights around the world. The *New York Times* quoted Timothy E. Wirth, a State Department counselor who oversees human rights policy, as saying this about human rights in the PRC: "Limited progress was made in 1993. More progress was made in early 1994." But, he added, "much more significant progress is going to be necessary" for China's preferred trading status to be extended.[7] How the Clinton administration responds to this report and continues to engage the PRC remains to be seen.

Should American foreign policy toward the PRC be predicated on human rights being sufficiently improved as a condition for continuing free trade with that country? Should this be the most important priority in our relations with the PRC? If not, how should the United States conduct its relations with the PRC?

The United States might adopt a nuanced policy, striving to achieve a number of foreign policy objectives simultaneously: making economic reform in the PRC and improving trade and investment relations with the United States a major concern for both countries; creating an Asia-Pacific regional security system based on sharing defense and weapons information and on adherence to international agreements that limit weapons proliferation; and improving human rights, with accountability being established through private or third-party inspections. While pressing hard to liberalize economic relations, the United States should continue to negotiate separately on the other two objectives as well. The subtle connections that link all three areas together will invariably be strengthened.

Insisting that human rights be improved or favorable trade status will be withdrawn defeats our goal of encouraging greater marketization and economic development in the PRC and might delay the improvement of human rights. Moreover, such linkage is not appropriate at a time when the leaders of the PRC face three formidable challenges: First, they must respond to severe economic challenges and create a new socialist market system. Second, there are four decades of pent-up consumer demand from nearly 1.3 billion people who want to live like the people in Japan, South Korea, Hong Kong, or the Republic of China (ROC) on Taiwan. To meet this new consumer demand, the economy must perform efficiently with social peace and political stability. Third, Deng Xiaoping and many other top leaders are in their nineties. As no legal institutional means for a leadership transfer has ever been established in this regime, a fierce power struggle might erupt after Deng is gone.

Unless the PRC's leaders successfully meet these three challenges, their political system will be subject to severe stress and possible collapse. And if a new market system cannot be created to support the living standards the people want, political dissatisfaction could threaten social and political stability. Yet the Clinton administration is threatening trade sanctions unless the PRC leaders improve human rights sufficiently to satisfy the United States, while the PRC is trying desperately to solve its problems.

A better way would be for the United States to encourage the PRC to promote marketization and trade liberalization while negotiating separately with the PRC's leaders to improve human rights and reduce weapons proliferation. By negotiating these issues separately, the United States could achieve its goals and allow the PRC's leaders sufficient time to deal with their three major challenges. Can we justify this nonlinkage foreign policy by the United States toward the PRC? I believe the answer is yes; the PRC is already evolving in new directions that hold great promise for the long-term improvement of human rights and welfare, issues that have a profound bearing on the PRC and its Asian neighbors.

These new directions now under way in the PRC are best understood by comparing the PRC with the smaller Chinese state across the Taiwan Straits, the ROC. Such a comparison strongly suggests that time is on the side of the United States if its leaders and Congress can be more patient while adopting the negotiation strategy suggested above.

CAN HISTORY TEACH US ANYTHING?

George Santayana once said that "those who cannot remember the past are condemned to repeat it." Although this may be true, there is the additional problem of agreeing about what kind of history has taken place before we can worry about what history is worth remembering. In the case of twentieth-century Chinese history, the simple facts appear to be these.

In 1949 China divided into two separate states, or political entities, each having its own constitution and government; these entities held different visions of history, pursued different goals, and selected different means to achieve those goals. They had been at war since the spring of 1927, when their earlier coalition, formed to overthrow China's warlords, suddenly fell apart. Chiang Kai-shek, one of the powerful leaders of the Kuomintang (Nationalist party, or KMT), decided to eliminate the Communist party by a series of violent attacks (he did, however, allow communist members to renounce their cause and join the KMT). Thereafter, these two parties fought bitterly to win the support of the Chinese people and unify China under their rule. By the end of 1945, when the war with Japan ended, both parties braced for a final struggle. By the fall of 1949, the Communist party and its military forces had defeated the KMT and its military, forcing KMT government and military refugees (probably around 1.5 million) to flee to Taiwan.

Between December 1949 and June 1950, because of a mounting Communist buildup that certainly would have taken over Taiwan, the great Chinese civil war seemed to be over. The outbreak of the Korean War, however, was an accident of history that greatly influenced the course of Chinese history. American military intervention prevented the PRC from attacking Taiwan and made it impossible for Chiang Kai-shek's forces to mount an attack on the PRC without American consent.

After 1950, these two Chinese states and their societies chose divergent paths of development.[8] Although each state claimed to represent China, neither admitted the existence of the other. But in the spring of 1992, the ROC National Assembly convened in Taipei and agreed to end the ROC's state of war with the PRC, thus affirming its existence, and to hold national elections on Taiwan for central government leaders of the ROC. The latter decision meant that the ROC leaders affirmed the independence of the ROC state while still claiming to represent China. The PRC leaders, however, still claim Taiwan as a "runaway province" and refuse to recognize the ROC as a political entity that might have diplomatic relations with nations that have formal ties with the PRC. But let us return to the two nations' divergent paths of development, which will help us understand the current situation in the PRC.

THE ROC MODERNIZATION EXPERIENCE

After 1949 the KMT confronted two major threats: (1) a takeover by the PRC through internal subversion, fomenting socioeconomic opposition and promoting revolution and (2) an overseas Taiwan nationalist revolutionary movement. Having rebuilt its party by late 1952, the KMT decided on two great missions: (1) mounting an anticommunist crusade to save Chinese civilization and retake the mainland from communist rule; (2) establishing a new society on Taiwan based on party founder Sun Yat-sen's doctrine, the Three Principles of the People. This doctrine called for building a sovereign nation based on constitutional-democratic governance and a high level of economic prosperity based on a relatively equal distribution of wealth and income but associated with an economic system of private property and a free market.

Given these tasks, the new KMT decided that it must not allow any political parties to form and compete until the conditions were appropriate for a political marketplace. To that end, the government would deal harshly with critics trying to delegitimize the ROC polity; democracy would be promoted at the local government level by allowing free elections; and the party would uphold the ROC constitution approved in 1947 for the government on Taiwan. The KMT and the ROC government, therefore, strongly adhered to these political rules until 1986, when KMT chairman and ROC president Chiang Ching-kuo launched reforms to change these political rules and promote the new rules of democratization.

The ROC government, therefore, severely punished critics and opponents and maintained tight control over political life by such things as regulating the public media. Beyond these activities, the regime allowed households to educate their children, utilize the free market, enrich themselves, and live a free life. To develop Taiwan's economic welfare and a flourishing civil society, the party and government carried out three important reforms in the early 1950s: (1) land reform by redistributing property rights, expanding the number of households having private property, and recompensing former landowners; (2) providing education for all primary school-age children; (3) organizing local elections every three years for village head, city mayor and council, township leader, urban councils, and the Taiwan Provincial Council.

Building on Sun Yat-sen's ideas of allowing individuals to own property and manage their businesses, the KMT regime guided the marketplace through astute economic, fiscal, and monetary policies to encourage free enterprise while avoiding the pathologies of market failures and powerful, greedy businesspeople. At the same time, the KMT allowed a relatively free ideological marketplace to evolve as long as no one advocated Marxism or Leninist ideas to overthrow capitalism and individuals did not engage in political activity. Western liberalism soon competed with Sunist doctrine and Confucianistic humanism.

For many decades, then, the ROC enjoyed a prospering, free economic marketplace and a flourishing ideological marketplace while strictly adhering to political rules that forbade individuals to challenge the regime through organizing political parties, publishing ideas and criticism undermining the regime's legitimacy, or engaging in activities threatening political and social stability. By 1986, the KMT leadership decided that the time was appropriate for democratization. The dramatic changes in the eight years that followed represent the rapid political development to a limited democracy; in late 1996, elections for the nation's top leaders, president and vice-president, will take place, making the ROC a consolidated democracy.

THE PRC MODERNIZATION EXPERIENCE

With a large population and area to rule, the Communist party and government embarked on a very different road to modernization. The PRC's leaders were committed to building, as rapidly as possible, a society without private property in which collective forms of life embraced all production and distribution. To that end, the Communist party, by 1956, had destroyed the market economy, eliminated private property, and created new collective organizations for the people. The Communist party also silenced criticism and strictly controlled the ideological marketplace, allowing only the circulation of Marxist, Leninist, and Maoist ideas and writings. By establishing a new government and party bureaucracy of incredible size, this new polity soon invaded every nook and cranny of society. The three marketplaces of economics, ideas, and politics had been completely eliminated.

Not satisfied with this achievement, the party's paramount leader, Mao Tse-tung, continued to impose radical reforms on China's society, organizing larger forms of collective life to regiment and control individual life even more strictly. These reforms were associated with great mass movements to mobilize the population. The outcomes were horrific. Widespread famine occurred between 1958 and 1962. In 1966 the Communist party became severely divided when Mao took control and launched a Cultural Revolution, which so ruined the people's spirit and tore up the fabric of society that, by the time Mao died in September 1976, most of the older party leaders were willing to abandon Mao's dreams and policies and initiate reforms that gradually transformed Chinese society in a way that the party probably never intended.

THE BURDEN OF CHINA'S PAST

The PRC's population had almost doubled by 1980, but its socialist government had failed to create an efficient, modern economy. The inefficient block of iron, steel, machine tool, and other industries and services established decades earlier required complete upgrades in technology and capital to be competitive in the world market. The nation also wanted more consumer goods to improve people's living standards and to improve its enormous environmental problems, which had worsened over time.

These new developments could not be undertaken without an efficient market system. In the socialist economy of the past, the prices of goods and services did not reflect their true scarcity values or produce the correct price signals to enable firms to allocate their resources efficiently. Without legal private property rights, households lacked the economic incentives to work hard, save, invest, or manage their activities. Recognizing these difficulties, the Communist party leadership began experimenting with economic reforms after 1980 to correct these dysfunctions. By fits and starts the

economic reforms continued, but not until November 1992 did the
Communist party's leadership finally commit to building a new market
system with socialist features.

This commitment opened up a great debate over what the new
market system should be. Meanwhile, the Chinese people, from top
to bottom, seized the opportunity to strive for greater freedom,
acquire wealth, and realize their ambitions. Slowly, a new economic
system formed. Official figures, which greatly understate the
organizational changes over the last few years, suggest that the old
structure of state enterprises and collectives has gradually declined
because joint ven-tures between Chinese and foreign firms and
privately managed enterprises have increased. More important, the
hybrid forms created by officials, collectives, and state-private firms
have mushroomed in the last few years.[9]

The current reforms will continue if the PRC's huge party-state
bureaucracy is rolled back and the people acquire new habits of trust,
compliance with contracts, and adherence to the law. A large
bureaucracy and widespread corruption are legacies of the past:
namely, the failed policies of the 1956–1992 period and the bad
habits they produced among the people. Only a continual opening
up of the PRC's market economy can create the ferment and
innovation to promote new market habits, loosen bureaucratic
control, and allow subcounty organizations to expand and manage
their affairs freely. Changing human habits and reducing bureaucracy
greatly depend on market enhancement, particularly greater
domestic market integration linked to the outside world and the U.S.
economy. As more American imports circulate within the PRC,
consumer tastes and habits will change, just as they did when the
PRC began importing Taiwan's products in the late 1980s.

Much of the current outcry in China over corruption is because
of the lack of markets, clear property rights, and laws for contracting
and enforcing contracts. As more markets and new laws emerge, the
corruption people rage against will diminish. But the PRC's economic
legacy still casts a shadow over the Chinese people, who struggle to
do business in primitive markets without clearly defined property
rights and laws to protect those rights.

Another important legacy of China's past that afflicts the
intellectuals and the elite is utopianism, which has always been a

powerful element of Chinese thinking.[10] Mao Tse-tung was a utopian. China's tragic leap into socialism in the 1950s and the violent events that followed owed much to Mao and the Communist party's utopian outlook, and its insidious influence exists even today. Many student-worker leaders of the spring 1989 democratic movement thought, spoke, and acted in a utopian way, arrogantly demanding that the Communist party make unrealistic and impractical reforms. The folksinger Chang Kuang-t'ien is cashing in on the recent commercial success of Mao-type products, criticizing the Communist party for downplaying "the Mao that matters most, the Mao who tried to give China what it has lacked for 5,000 years—a spiritual basis. And that was the Mao of the Cultural Revolution."[11] Such utopian thinking seems prevalent among the youth of today's PRC.

Another shared Chinese value is a strong propensity for this-worldliness, largely because the Chinese lack a religion that depicts an afterlife (except Buddhism). The Chinese attach enormous importance to their allotted lifetimes. Committed to realizing their personal goals in the present, the average Chinese allocates most of her or his energy to solo-type activities in the strong hope that such activities will produce spectacular results. These expectations reinforce the belief that other parties, including the government, will deliver as they promise. Such expectations can put Chinese society at risk; any sudden collapse of those expectations immediately produces public outrage toward political authority. The present danger for Beijing's leaders is that, if people do not experience substantive improvements in their living standards in the near future, widespread discontent might erupt to threaten public security.

Those living in Beijing during the spring of 1989 observed the enormous crowds that quickly formed in city streets; they realized how difficult it would be for the authorities to maintain public order if such crowds became enraged. Similar incidents could precipitate a political crisis; leaders then blame each other for the mess. A divided leadership inevitably causes power struggle.

But a more disquieting connection exists among traditional Chinese utopianism, rising expectations, and the tenuous state of public order in China. Chinese intellectuals and elite have always threatened the Chinese political center; their inflammatory writings in books, newspapers, and journals criticized, scolded, insulted, and attacked China's leaders and demanded that they step down or adopt major reforms. China has a long history of such activity.

The outpouring of writings both inside and outside China between 1900 and 1910 aroused popular anger toward the Manchu government and strongly contributed to the uprisings that toppled that government in 1911. Intellectual writings that called for the nation's leaders to take action toward the foreign powers and rebuff Japanese imperialism played an important role in mobilizing the huge student street demonstrations of May 1919, quickly supported by city merchants and businessmen. Intellectual writings in the 1920s fueled the strong nationalistic sentiments that ejected the foreign powers from China. In the 1930s and 1940s, angry writings in journals, novels, short stories, and newspaper articles stirred popular passions, especially of the youth, and criticized and condemned the ruling authorities for failing the people. In 1947–1948 many elites and intellectuals withdrew their support from the Nationalist government and turned to the Communist party. The majority of these critics shared the utopian belief that Chinese society could be cured of its ills if only a different group of leaders ruled the country.

Realizing the power of the pen, the Communist party always tightly controlled the public media. Experience had taught the Communist party that when intellectual magazines appeared, political opposition soon followed, leading to street demonstrations and crowds demanding that authorities change their policies or give up power. China never had a tradition of constructive moderate criticism, and China's leaders have never tolerated widespread popular dissent. Gradual economic development, however, can improve the living standards and life chances of the people. Moreover, if an ideological marketplace of ideas gradually follows, as it did in the ROC on Taiwan, such a marketplace could serve to dampen shrill utopianism by allowing for more rational discourse. In fact, an embryonic ideological marketplace formed in the mid-1980s in the PRC and continues to grow. But the regime's powerful internal security control system still limits its healthy development.

After 1992, the long-term, divergent developmental trajectories of the PRC and ROC began to converge; the PRC is moving inexorably toward a new economic marketplace based on more hybrid organizational forms, and an embryonic ideological marketplace is slowly expanding. Even the Communist party is no longer like the Leninist organization of old except in organizational form. Most of its members are no longer strongly committed to building a socialist system, and some grope for a new ideological formula as to what the party's new objectives should be.

Yet the Communist party still practices "hard authoritarianism," relying on a vast police and security system to maintain strong control over critics and any potential opposition movements. In this respect the PRC increasingly resembles the ROC on Taiwan during the 1950s and 1960s, when an economic and ideological marketplace had formed but the regime opposed the creation of a political marketplace.

As relations across the Taiwan Straits improve, the ROC modernization experience continues to exercise a powerful influence on intellectual and elite circles of the mainland. They now recognize that the KMT regime on Taiwan produced an economic and political miracle. Whether they give sufficient credit for that achievement to Sunist doctrine is another matter. Taiwan-style modernization is spreading slowly on the mainland. Its mature development will require more time, and there are bound to be differences in how the three new marketplaces take form. But that process now seems irreversible. How can the PRC learn from the ROC modernization experience and develop a new economic marketplace?

LESSONS FOR THE PRC

In November 1992 the Communist party affirmed that it was establishing a state-guided market system, and journals and newspapers now debate how this economic market should be organized and by what rules. The PRC government must decide, as did the ROC, on the desired mixture of private, public, and other property rights and what laws should govern the ownership and management of different forms of property rights. Once these property rights and their laws are agreed on, the PRC authorities must establish the complementary legal system of courts, judges, and lawyers to enforce and uphold these laws. But these reforms can logically flow only from some agreement as to what the desired

mixture of property rights is to be. Once that has been decided, the
PRC government can then identify and value private, public, and
mixed property forms by undertaking surveys that

- Identify the different forms of property and classify them
  according to law
- Record relevant information about property owners and
  the kinds of property they own
- Assess a current market value for these types of property
- Assess a fair tax as a percentage of the property's current
  market value

Then the PRC must establish the institutions and organizations to

- Set procedures for periodically reassessing property taxes
- Establish laws permitting property owners to contract
  with each other for the purpose of profit making
- Establish laws permitting property owners to transfer or
  sell their property
- Establish laws to protect property owners

To my knowledge, none of the above activities has been carried
out nationwide or experimentally. Yet they are the necessary building
blocks for developing a new market system. Until some mixture of
private-public property rights is agreed on and these rights valued,
taxed, and protected, the PRC leaders and people must endure
corruption, inefficiency, and fragmented markets. The nation will be
unable to have an efficient, modern fiscal system based on law. State
and local governments will not be able to obtain sufficient revenue
as economic development advances; property owners will lack the
incentives to manage their property efficiently and profitably.

Future PRC-U.S. Trade Relations

Economic and ideological marketplaces gradually formed and then
flourished in the ROC over a forty-year period; the PRC now inches
toward this same development. Because conditions on the mainland
and Taiwan are very different, the transition to these new

marketplaces on the mainland only began a little more than ten years ago and will require another decade or more before they evolve as they did on Taiwan. The historical transition to these marketplaces is still little understood and should not be unduly hastened either by enthusiasts or by outsiders.

U.S. leaders and politicians should realize that for a long period Taiwan's modernization experience diverged from that of the mainland but that both Chinese societies are now gradually converging. U.S. policy can nurture a beneficial marketplace development sequence in the PRC if Washington negotiates with Beijing on an issue-by-issue basis rather than linking, say, trade and human rights issues. By promoting the Taiwan-style modernization pattern in the PRC, U.S. foreign policy could help the PRC develop a new economic marketplace based on more private property rights and hybrid property forms and encourage the PRC government to allow an ideological marketplace to debate and legitimate the new economic marketplace.

The PRC already is a key economic player in APEC, and stable prosperous foreign trade is as important for the PRC as it is for other APEC members. Enhancing trade between the PRC and other APEC members, particularly the United States, should be one of America's top priorities in its foreign affairs with the PRC. Linking PRC trade sanctions to nontrade objectives is a bad idea for the United States and other APEC members.

The volume of trade and foreign investment between the PRC and the United States has already grown rapidly; such trade is inextricably linked with Taiwan and Hong Kong's foreign trade. U.S. trade sanctions such as refusing to grant the PRC most-favored nation status will increase duties and elevate prices by as much as one-third of the PRC imports into the United States, which would force the PRC to limit U.S. imports. In 1991 the Hong Kong Trade Development Council estimated that, if the United States removed the PRC's MFN status, "Hong Kong's external trade might be reduced by 5 to 7 percent with a reduction in its GDP as much as 1.3 to 1.8 percentage points."[12] Therefore, these actions would cause enormous anxiety in East and Southeast Asia and eventually harm the rapid economic growth under way there.

If the PRC refuses to liberalize its markets, the United States can apply the same pressures and trade sanctions it used successfully between 1985 and 1992 on South Korea to open its markets.[13]

Meanwhile, the United States should press the PRC to improve human rights on an issue-by-issue basis. Americans have good reasons to be unhappy with the way the PRC government has treated its political prisoners and managed a huge penal system producing commodities that often find their way into the U.S. market. But some of these issues already have been negotiated on an issue-by-issue basis between Beijing and Washington, with progress achieved. As mentioned at the outset, the Red Cross soon will inspect PRC prisons. To be sure, the progress never seems rapid or substantial enough to satisfy those groups greatly concerned about those problems. But U.S. promises of loans or economic aid and moral suasion will encourage Beijing's leaders to give those problems attention. In fact, by intensifying economic contacts with the PRC, the United States can still strongly insist on human rights improvement, a policy the Clinton administration appeared to be enacting in late January 1994.[14] This is the nonlinkage approach argued above, and I hope that the Clinton administration will stay the course.

Having experienced enormous change in the last fifteen years, the PRC is now at a historical crossroads: it can move as the ROC on Taiwan did some thirty years ago, or it can resist reform and risk political power struggle, political upheaval, and collapse. Such chaos would have serious repercussions on bordering nations and threaten much of the new global economy. The PRC government needs time to carry out a property rights reform, to integrate its domestic markets, and to develop a modern fiscal and monetary system so that inflation can be controlled and modern economic growth sustained. These reforms might be derailed if the U.S. government resorts to retaliatory trade policies to achieve other foreign policy goals. The reforms must continue. If the PRC can promote greater domestic market integration and absorb more U.S. imports, the Chinese leaders and elite might just be able to affirm those other two important marketplaces needed to improve human rights: the intellectual and political marketplaces, which represent full-blown modernization.

NOTES

1. Susan Awanohara, "Breathing Space: Clinton Delays on Conditions to China's MFN Renewal," *Far Eastern Economic Review*, June 10, 1993, p. 13.
2. *New York Times*, October 1, 1993, p. A6.
3. R. W. Apple, "No Progress Seen as Clinton Meets with China's Chief," *New York Times*, November 20, 1993, p. 1. The United States had agreed on November 19 to sell a sophisticated $8 million supercomputer to the PRC as an incentive to win Beijing's concessions for improving human rights.
4. Patrick E. Tyler, "Beijing Will Take Steps on Rights, Bush Is Told," *New York Times*, January 17, 1994, p. A2.
5. Patrick E. Tyler, "Red Cross Says the Chinese Are Seriously Discussing Prison Visits," *New York Times*, January 22, 1994, p. 3.
6. Thomas L. Friedman, "China to Allow Foreign Banks Greater Access," *New York Times*, January 22, 1994, p. 1.
7. Steven Greenhouse, "China's Human Rights Record Is Denounced by the State Dept." *New York Times*, February 2, 1994, p. A4.
8. For a review of these divergent trajectories, see Ramon H. Myers, ed., *Two Societies in Opposition: The Republic of China and the People's Republic of China after Forty Years* (Stanford: Hoover Institution Press, 1991).
9. For a discussion of this development, see Ni Chi-hsiang, "Kuan-yu wo-kuo lun-ho suo-chih hsing-shih ti hsien-chuang, wen-t'i ho chien-i" ("Some Problems and Opinions about Our Nation's Mixed Property Forms and Their Conditions") *Kai-ko* (*Reform*), no. 3 (1993): 40–45.
10. For a good discussion of the importance of utopianism in Chinese history, see Thomas A. Metzger, "The Sociological Imagination in China: Comments on the Thought of Chin Yao-chi (Ambrose Y. C. King)," *Journal of Asian Studies* 52, no. 4 (November 1993): 937–48. See particularly the list of references related to Metzger's writings on p. 948.
11. Matei Mihaica, "The Pied Piper of Peking," *Far Eastern Economic Review*, September 30, 1993, p. 55.
12. James T. H. Tang, "Hong Kong's International Status," *Pacific Review* 6, no. 3 (1993): 213.
13. Jongryn Mo and Ramon H. Myers, eds., *Shaping a New Economic Relationship: The Republic of Korea and the United States* (Stanford: Hoover Institution Press, 1993).
14. See Thomas L. Friedman, "New Tack on China," *New York Times*, January 23, 1994, p. 8.